THE UNPROTECTED MARRIAGE

CHRIS NORA

The characters and events portrayed in this book are fictitious. Any similarity to real persons, living or dead, is coincidental and not intended by the author.

ISBN: 9798360250708

DEDICATION

This book is dedicated to God Almighty and to my family.

CONTENTS

ACKNOWLEDGMENTS

My acknowledgement goes to God almighty for his inspiration, strength and privilege given to me.

INTRODUCTION

The term unprotected means exposure, lack of protection. Wherever lack of protection exists, it means there is no security there. Marriage as a union between two (2) people (Man and Woman) as partners in a personal relationship, is supposed to be a united relationship at that moment the man and the woman agreed to become partners. But the moment the both partners fail to be submissive to one another, insecurity encrypts into the marriage and makes the marriage an unprotected marriage.

LOVE IN MARRIAGE

It all starts with a smile, a gaze, a few moments of flirty conversations, real intimacy because when you were newly married, all you could think about was how amazing and romantic it was to be together but as time passed, you got so accustomed to so many habits that you even stopped wooing each other or making any special efforts. The truth remains that every marriage has bumps that can come up anytime, but what's important is passing through them with courage & wisdom and learning from your past mistakes in order to enjoy a better married life. It is said that he who finds a wife, finds a good thing and obtains favor from the Lord, this implies that marriage is a beautiful thing, but out of ignorance we lose the beauty of our marriages. Ignorance has made most people lose their healthy marriage by the inability to understand the difference between protection and possession. Most healthy marriages were destroyed by being possessive of their partner while thinking they are protecting their marriage. Possessiveness in marriage has become a very big challenge to most marriages today. When someone is Possessive about you, they control you, dominate you and rob you of your freedom, but when Protective of you, they make sure that you are fine, check up on you and make you feel loved and wanted. Love in marriage could mean sharing the house load with your partner, taking turns to do the dishes, cooking a meal, sharing finances, getting the children ready for school, making sacrifices for the other's happiness and much more. Love plays a crucial role in a marriage and evolves as time goes by. Undoubtedly, there's nothing more beautiful than having someone hold your hand till the end of time, and with the right balance of intimacy, a marriage is bound to last for a lifetime. After the initial rush of passion when newly married, love is supposed to be strengthened and transforms into an unbreakable bond. Marriage emotional intimacy is a feeling of closeness to your partner. When you're emotionally intimate with your partner, you can share personal feelings and easily know that they will understand you completely, as you display affection without fear of being dismissed or judged harshly. Couples who know how to effectively and openly communicate with each other, experience fulfilled marriage, but on the other hand, those who don't, are likely to experience a buildup of anger, frustration and resentment. When was the last time you thought about how healthy your marriage was? It's important that you do all you can to save your marriage and keep it happy and healthy, therefore, it's essential for both partners to pay due attention to their marriage to identify their latent issues and resolve them before they worsen due to lack of attention. Sometimes most people ought to know the right thing to do, yet they allow ignorance to ruin their marriage. Being in a marriage with someone who doesn't value you will lead to repeated breaches of trust which deteriorate the quality of the marriage. As the scripture says, both of you must be submissive to one another, therefore, relationship marriage is a basis for cooperation, trust, respect, responsibility and problem solving which as a result make both partners to be transparent to each other and never to hide anything from one another. Trying to make a perfect marriage by putting too many restrictions and expecting only your partner to abide by the rules, is an act of possessiveness which will only create a gap between you and your partner. Possessiveness in any marriage can turn a healthy marriage into a toxic one as it gives room for cheating, lies and broken promises which can severely damage the trust between couples and triggers insecurity.

INSECURITY IN MARRIAGE

Insecurity is a feeling of inadequacy that is born out of a lack of self-confidence. It can cause you to doubt your abilities, instincts in marriage, making it difficult for you to believe in yourself and to trust others. Being insecure in a marriage can be addicting, the more you entertain the thoughts, the bigger the insecurity becomes hereby making you to be possessive of your partner. The cause of insecurities in any marriage is often as a result of lack of self- love, when you hold a harmful belief against your partner, or afraid of failure, or you can't be able to trust completely. Insecurity sometimes is as a result of our painful past and mistakes, social experiences, adult relationships, personality factors, and mental health conditions. If you don't trust your partner, jealousy will likely take over your interactions with that person, making it impossible to believe anything they say or do. Insecurity has made most men not to establish their wives, it has made most men to hide their worth from the woman they called their wife, it has made most men to treat their wives as a slave by depriving them of their marital rights. The question is, were you forced as a man to marry the woman you are living with? Does it mean you still don't know the woman you lived with for many years? The kind of life you live may cause you not to trust your partner, and until you resist such a lifestyle, you will never trust yourself, your partner, or your instincts in marriage.

POSSESSIVENESS IN MARRIAGE

No one would want to be possessive in marriage if the consequences are well understood. Some people fake their love, confidence and trust in a marriage, but as time goes by, it triggers insecurity because you can't fake love for so long when you don't really love. Love is not to be acted but to be expressed because love is a strong feeling of affection, protectiveness, and respect for one another. No one wants to be insecure in marriage due to its endless doubts, jealousy and hurt.

But sometimes when you see your partner befriends people of the opposite sex, or you may have seen a random text and calls from a friend you don't know, due to lack of trust, you allow Jealousy to inflict Insecurity which will make you become possessive of your partner while thinking you are protecting your marriage. Most men like's putting their wives in a tight corner by not providing for their needs but once the woman denies him of sex, they assumed that they are being put in a tight corner as if they have been faithful to their wives. What is the essence of buying a car for the woman you made a house wife when you don't like fueling the car each time she needs to go out? Your marriage becomes unprotected when you start feeling insecure. Insecurities can also be caused by comparing yourself with your partner's exes or feeling inferior to your partner's achievements. Insecurity has caused most people to be possessive of their partner which leads to the destruction of the love in their marriage. Sometimes you may not even realize that lack of self-love and self-esteem can cause insecurity which drags your romantic marriage relationship down. Marriages are destroyed today as a result of lack of Love, Trust, and Protection. Sometimes you may feel like your partner isn't telling you everything, or it might seem like there is much you don't know about him or her which he is unwilling to share, but the truth is that you can't trust someone right out of the box because trust can only be gained over a long period of time and once you have gained that trust, you need to ensure that you are keeping that trust. Just know that as a man, you are the head of the home and it is in your footsteps that your family is walking on. The questions are, will your footsteps lead them to the right track? Or will it lead them to the same evil lifestyles you are living? Are you the type of a man that compares your age to that of your wife, yet you can't still lead by example as the senior? Or are you the type that condemns your wife without teaching her the right way of doing those things you want her to be doing? Just know that quarreling without correction can not stop anyone from repeating the same mistakes. Therefore, if you can stop being possessive in your marriage and start being protective, you will always give corrections anytime anyone makes a mistake for human beings are bond to mistakes, by so doing, it will help both your wife and the children to learn how to own up their mistakes and avoid constant repetition of a certain act.

SEX IN MARRIAGE

How do you view sex in a marriage? What do you aim at when having sex with your partner? Do you have sex just because you want to make offspring's or do you have sex just to satisfy your urge? Sex in marriage should be an act of intimacy that not just strengthens the marital relationship but also help to convey love, attraction, or commitment for both partners. The way you picture sex with your partner affects your behavior towards the person, and make you to respect the feelings of that person.

Sex is not to be abused, therefore, the frequency of sex in that marriage depends on your partner personal emotions and level of fulfillment. The quality of sex that married people have can get influenced by their marital conflicts. Many married couples suffer from various sex issues that affect their marriage and can even impact its survival. Most men maltreat even their children whenever they couldn't get sex from their partner, this is because sex is seen as an act of just satisfying self-urge in that marriage. That is the reason why most men get angry whenever they can't have sex with their partner, despite they have not been faithful to her. Like I said earlier, sex in a marriage is an act of intimacy that not just strengthens the marital relationship, but also help to convey love, attraction, or commitment for both partners. Therefore, both the husband and the wife must be in the mood before the aim of sex in that marriage as mentioned above can be achieved. Were there sex issues when newly married? The answer is NO. Then why would sex become an issue affecting the marriage now? That is because everything has changed totally from how it all started. It is true that each person's sexuality and sex drive are different along with their daily lives and activities, but that does not change the fact that love conquers all. When the love in any marriage dies, various factors come into play to decide the usual frequency of sex in that marriage. You realize that a lot has changed because you have deviated from how it was when newly married, kindly return back to the beginning when there is much Love, Trust, Care, and Attention. Both couples must be submissive to each other to avoid allowing insecurity to creep into their marriage, when that is done, achieving a healthy home won't be a difficult task again.

HOW DO YOU GAIN TRUST

You can gain trust by doing the right thing even when no one is looking because it's take's only a minute to get a crush on someone, an hour to like someone and a day to love someone but it takes a lifetime to forget someone. Sometimes you would find it extremely difficult to do the right thing, sometimes taking the wrong road is easier but you have to keep on making the difficult choice one after the other to stop insecurities from creeping into your marriage. If you feel like your partner has a hard time trusting you, or telling you the truth, it will affect the love you have for the person because when you don't trust your partner to do the right thing when you are not looking, then you are insecure of that person. Trust in any marriage can be broken by not maintaining promises, withholding love and affection, and not taking responsibility for inexcusable behavior.

IS IT POSSIBLE TO OVERCOME INSECURITY IN MARRIAGE?

Although it's never easy, it is possible if you can have control over yourself, for we all have some battles that we need to overcome. Without you knowing how to deal with trust issues, you would never be able to have a happy and fulfilling marriage because marriage paranoia drives a wedge between partners. We all deserve love, therefore, always give your partner the love, trust and protection they deserve. If you are having a lack of self-love, remember, before anyone can accept and love you, you should love and believe in yourself. If you feel disconnected, or frustrated about the state of your marriage or you think that you can no longer control your thoughts, talk to someone responsible or seek help from a counselor.

CAN A BROKEN TRUST BE REBUILT AGAIN?

Breaking trust is like breaking a glass which assembling them again will take real honesty and strength from both partners. If you are the one that broken Trust, know that if your partner is willing to forgive you, it's going to be a long road to recovery because it won't be easy for you but just remember that it's going to be even more difficult for them, therefore, you need to make a Choice and take a Chance for a Change. If you are the one that Trust has been broken, know that by giving a second chance you may be setting yourself up to be hurt again but if you are willing to try, here are the three (3) things you will look for in your partner. ACKNOWLEDGEMENT: Does your partner acknowledge their mistakes? Do they genuinely feel bad over their mistakes? Or do they feel bad because they are caught? Have it in mind that you can't change what you can't see, if they are not open and honest, then it is time you move on but if they genuinely acknowledge their mistakes, then look for commitment in them. COMMITMENT: Is your partner committed to change? Or is the commitment short-lived? Change is not easy and requires real commitment to achieve. If they are not committed, then it's time you move on but if they are committed, then look for consistency. CONSISTENCY: It only takes a moment to break trust but it can take a lifetime to rebuild it. Consistency is the key to show that change is permanent, if your partner is not consistent then move on but if they genuinely acknowledge their mistakes, committed to change and show consistency, then give them a chance because your painful encounters may have been the turning point you need to create a home that is better than ever.

ADVICE

It's true that we don't know what we've gotten until we lose it, but it's also true that we don't know what we've been missing until it arrives. Love comes to those who still hope, although they have been disappointed, to those who still believe, although they have been betrayed, to those who still need to love, although they have been hurt before, and to those who have courage and faith to build trust again. Sometimes the best way to appreciate someone is to put yourself in their shoes. We can get so used to certain things being done for us that we even stop to notice them, it could be as simple as getting the kids ready for school, taking out the trash, making sure everyone has home cooked food or dealing with endless piles of laundry. We get preoccupied that we stopped noticing the people helping us to get ahead, but a little acknowledgement can go a long way. The law of karma shows us that every action has an equal and opposite reaction, therefore, how people treat you is their karma and how you respond is yours. Whenever we are acting in a certain way, we are equally attracting them back into our lives, although we don't always receive the same pains from the same person, we give it to but it always comes back even if through another person, but the biggest challenge is that we never understand the pain we caused someone until someone else causes the same pain to us. It's important to make the right decision in a marriage but we should never be dismissive of our partner’s emotions. We can end something if we need to but there's no need to undermine our partner's feelings in the process. Is a moment of happiness really worth causing your partner a lifetime hurt? Or is a few moments of temporal pleasure worth losing the person that you treasure? Instead of giving our attention to the outside world, let's make our partner feel like the center of our world. Always take care of that person that has been on your side from day one, complement them and appreciate their efforts. Just like flowers require water to keep them beautiful, people require Attention, Love, Honesty, Respect, Trust and Energy to keep them beautiful also. I hope you will find courage to make the right ***Choice*** and take a ***Chance*** for the ***Change*** you longed for.

www.ingramcontent.com/pod-product-compliance
Lightning Source LLC
LaVergne TN
LVHW020533160826
845677LV00015B/4041

* 9 7 9 8 3 6 0 2 5 0 7 0 8 *